WEIGHING IN

how to understand your body, lose weight, and live a healthier lifestyle

D1021855

Sylvie Boutaudou
illustrated by Laëtitia Aynié
edited by Melissa Daly

sunscreen

Book series design by Higashi Glaser Design
Production Manager: Jonathan Lopes

Library of Congress Cataloging-in-Publication Data:
Boutaudou, Sylvie.
Weighing in: how to understand your body, lose weight,
and live a healthier lifestyle / by Sylvie Boutaudou with Melissa Daly ;
illustrated by Laëtitia Aynié.
p. cm.–(Sunscreen)
Includes index.
Original French title: Marre de mes kilos en trop
ISBN 0-8109-9228-0
1. Obesity in adolescence—Juvenile literature. I. Daly, Melissa. II. Aynié, Laëtitia.
III. Title.

RJ399.C6B68 2005
618.92'398—dc22
2005011775

Translated by JMS Books. LLC

Published in 2006 by Amulet Books
an imprint of Harry N. Abrams, Incorporated
115 West 18th Street
New York, NY 10011
www.abramsbooks.com

Printed and bound in China
10 9 8 7 6 5 4 3 2 1

Abrams is a subsidiary of
LA MARTINIÈRE

contents

9   Introduction

phase 1:

OVERWEIGHT, UNDER HAPPY

12   i'm not obese, but . . .

13   sticks and stones . . .

15   just a joke?

18   why is it so hard to defend myself?

20   don't take it!

22   we don't want him on our team!

24   i don't look the part

26   life of the party

28   mall rats

31   being left out . . . or leaving yourself out?

32   impossible standards

34   the feminine ideal

37   not man enough

40   what about romance?

44   your family pretends not to see

46   no one takes me seriously

50   your family never lets you forget

52   making your own decisions

phase 2:
HOW I GOT TO BE SO HEAVY

56 the body mass index

58 the differences between boys
    and girls

60 a weighty past

62 it's not fair

64 a thousand temptations

68 the choice is yours

69 snack foods can be dangerous

71 not enough moving around

76 don't sweat the big stuff

phase 3:
HOW TO LOSE WEIGHT

80   getting help

82   what if they don't help?

85   who can help?

87   not a diet, but a lifestyle change

88   support and encouragement

90   the rules

94   how to deal with cravings

96   talk to your friends

98   get moving!

101 it worked! now what?

104 suggestions for further reading

106 index

WHY CAN'T I BE THIN? WHEN WILL I LOSE THIS BABY FAT? HOW DO I LOOK IN THESE JEANS? WHY DOES EVERYONE JUDGE ME BY MY BODY? WHY AM I OVERWEIGHT?

You've Got Enough on Your Plate

If only you could erase some words from the dictionary. Like "fat." Wouldn't that be great? It's such a hurtful word and it can make you feel ashamed and excluded. Of course, you have a few good friends who always stick by you and make you feel good about yourself. But still, as you all grow up, things change, and maybe it's starting to feel like something is alienating you from others. Gym class, parties, shopping for new clothes—all the simple things that come so easily for everyone else now seem like such a nightmare. And when you think about the opposite sex—something that's likely happening more and more often— it's easy to get depressed. Some days you'd rather just stay under the covers. You think: If only I could fit into my jeans, everything would be so much better, right?

I don't look the part

I'M NOT OBESE, BUT...

The feminine ideal

not man enough

IMPOSSIBLE STANDARDS

sticks and stones . . .

life of the party

OVERWEIGHT,

UNDER HAPPY

YOUR FAMILY
PRETENDS
NOT TO SEE

Your family
never lets you
forget

i'm not obese,
but . . .

Everyone's seen or heard about the TV shows on obese children who weigh 250 pounds at the age of twelve. Boys and girls with that kind of weight problem need medical attention. They often have difficulty walking and breathing, they can't run, and some of them have gotten to the point where they can no longer even go to school. In order to lose weight and have a normal life, they often have no other choice than to spend time in a special clinic. This book isn't meant for anyone with this kind of condition.

You know that your extra weight is nowhere near that catastrophic. The little roll of flab that shows underneath your sweater would never be the subject of a television documentary (not an interesting one, anyway). Nevertheless, it's enough to set you apart as the "chubby" kid in class, and you suffer for it.

sticks and
stones. . .

Your weight would not be such a big deal if everyone else didn't make such a big deal of it. Unfortunately, others don't need x-ray vision to see your waist size through your clothes. And the comments overweight kids endure, day in and day out, can sometimes be unbearable.

You know it only too well, right? Those words sting at the time, but then continue to ache for days as you repeat them to yourself over and over. You can't get them out of your head. It's the little comments here and there, or the insults thrown at you during an argument. No matter what part of the country you're in, the vocabulary is pretty much the same: chubby, big-boned, heavy . . . FAT.

If the goal of name-calling is to hurt someone, it works well. "I had a problem with a friend because I sort of messed up her bike," says twelve-year-old Naomi. "She was really mad and she yelled, 'That fatso squashed my bike,' before I could even explain. My weight had nothing to do with it! But even though I was really mad, I couldn't think of anything to say."

Naomi has pointed out exactly what is so annoying about these kinds of situations: Weight usually has nothing to do with it. You're having a simple discussion (or, OK, an argument) and just when you least expect it, the person throws the "fat thing" at you.

You spend plenty of time thinking about your weight, but fortunately you manage to forget about it sometimes, like Naomi did when she returned the bike to her friend. So when a comment like that is made, it proves to you that everyone else is always thinking about your weight, too. It's as if they've labeled you as "the fat kid" and are ready to remind you of your title at any given moment. Even if they do see beyond that under normal circumstances (people say a lot of things they don't mean in the heat of an argument), it still hurts. It's painful because you feel like your appearance puts up a veil between you and everyone else, and this veil keeps them from seeing who you really are. Also, unlike the weak spots of other kids—depression, low self-esteem, trouble in school—yours are visible to everyone all the time.

When you're overweight, your classmates know that you are unhappy about those extra pounds, and when they're angry and want to lash out, they go right for your sore spot on purpose.

just a joke?

When the insults start flying, it's tempting to fight back and send a few zingers of your own. You sure have enough of them stored up! But when it comes to a practical joke or a comment that makes everyone else laugh, it gets tricky. You don't want to seem like you're super-sensitive or you can't take a joke, so sometimes you just grin and bear it. Before the end of class one day, eleven-year-old Mary heard a classmate say "Could you roll yourself over here and hand me that eraser?" Everyone, even her best friend, started giggling. Mary didn't know what to do, so she gave her the eraser and did a lot of crying when she got home that day.

Ever since her last summer vacation, thirteen-year-old Gail no longer likes softball. During games, there was always some smart aleck making a comment to a friend like "What's she doing on the team—shouldn't she be going out for wrestling? She'd crush 'em!" while looking straight at Gail. Making fun of other people's imperfections is always meant to get a few laughs, but the person who's the butt of the joke never knows quite how to react. Jokes made at someone else's expense can be a kind of verbal abuse. It's a very aggressive gesture, and it can be even harder to deal with than an outright insult. If every-

one laughs, then the joke has been successful and the joker gets one up on you. Even worse, everyone else seems to be on his side and no one will come to your defense. Which of course motivates him to continue, not necessarily because he hates you, but because it makes him look cool.

Adults used to advise kids to just ignore this kind of thing. They said that if you ignore a bully, he'll eventually get bored and stop harassing you. But as you've probably realized, that doesn't always work. Sometimes you have to stand up for yourself. But you don't have to do it in such a way that lets the joker know he got to you, or that makes you look lame in front of the other kids. Instead, try using your own sense of humor to your advantage.

One boy named Damion has a catch-phrase that he brings out whenever he's given a hard time for being overweight: "At least I can go on a diet, but you'll always be stupid." Or he says, "Oh, a fat joke—I've never heard those before. Real original."

By saying things like this, Damion backs his abuser up against the wall. What Damion's really saying is: "You think you're attacking who I am, but you've really only made a comment about my appearance. On the other hand, you come off looking worse because you've acted like a jerk, which is never attractive."

why is it so hard to defend
myself?

Maybe you're not quick enough to fight back in time, like Damion. Maybe you've even completely lost it once or twice and cried in front of everyone after an especially mean or unexpected insult. It might be a bad memory for you, but think about it: The person who knocked you down to raise himself up did it in front of everyone—and it might not have made him look as cool as he thought. Chances are, the other kids knew he went over the line. He can still continue to make what he thinks are jokes, but you can rest assured that people see him for the not-very-nice person that he is, even if they don't always let you know they feel that way.

It might also be helpful to understand why you're so deeply affected by remarks about your weight. The reality is you feel guilty, so you hang your head and think, "He's right. I am too fat and it is my own fault." Many people think, like you probably do, that weight problems happen simply because you can't help but eat too much. The truth is that there are many causes (genetics and family eating habits, to name a few), some of which have nothing to do with you. The stereotypical fat person, like the one you see in movies or cartoons, is lazy, lies around in bed, doesn't like sports, and has no restraint. Fat people just eat buttercream cupcakes all day long, right? People think if you're fat, then it's all your fault. Our society values traits like determination, self-control, and ambition—basically the opposites of those fat people are stereo-typed by.

So, for example, when you're running track in gym class, you get comments like "Hey, look who finally made it!" as you approach the fin-ish line, even though you've done your best to do all the laps.

If one of your classmates were to have an accident that left him limping, no one would ever criticize him for being too slow. But a person who's not slim is often seen as being responsible for his own problem, so no one is going to give him a break. That, in a nutshell, explains the logic behind all the insults. Unfortunately, certain body types carry cer-tain judgments—even though they may be far from true. Right from the start, anyone with a few extra pounds is considered lazy and weak.

don't take it!

No matter what, the thing NOT to do when being teased or insulted is to believe the things that are being said to you. The person saying them will sense it, and that will encourage them to continue. You start thinking you're responsible for your weight ("If only I hadn't eaten so much chocolate . . ."). And the fact that you might agree a little bit with the person makes it hard for you to argue with him. But remember this: Comments about someone's weight are a form of discrimination and you have the right to defend yourself against this injustice. It is not acceptable to criticize someone just because of their appearance. Tall, short, fat, thin, straight hair or curly, we are all different, and we all deserve to be treated with respect.

So, to deal with the abuse, you need to respond and turn the joke back onto the person who's trying to send it your way. If you've already tried just blowing him off with a funny comment of your own and he's still going at it, you might need to get more serious. Say, "Hey, back off! You're annoying me and you're embarrassing yourself."

You can't wave a magic wand and change the way others see you, but you can at least have the satisfaction of not having taken it lying down. You might even be pleasantly surprised when some of the onlookers take your side. No one likes to see someone else being made fun of.

As you might already know, there is an even more unpleasant form of insult than the verbal kind. It's being left out. Your classmates have no trouble remembering you when they need help with their math homework, but when it comes to parties and other social events, they sidestep you completely. Sound familiar? Sometimes it's as if they don't even know you're there, other times they ignore you deliberately. If this is happening to you, you're probably convinced that it's those extra pounds that are causing the trouble. See if you can relate to the following real-life examples; they'll help you to understand why these things happen, how to deal with it and, most importantly, how to make it change.

we don't want him on
our team!

"Today we're playing basketball, so choose your teams." Those are the words twelve-year-old Joe hates to hear his gym teacher say more than anything. Like always, he'll be the last one chosen and, when he is, all the guys on his team will groan and make faces. The message is loud and clear: "If Joe is on our team, we're sure to lose." It's not the sort of response that's going to make him crazy about team sports. He plays, but only because he has to, not because he wants to. He actually used to love basketball just a few years ago. He even got his parents to put up a hoop in the driveway.

Just like Joe, you have probably abandoned an activity that you really like (swimming, football, softball . . .) because of someone's nasty remarks, or because you were afraid of not being as good as everyone else. It's completely understandable that you would feel that way, but think about what you lose by giving up something you like. Competing with others and being part of a team that is made up of people with different skill levels can be really fun and rewarding. This applies to other things besides sports, too. A teacher named Elisabeth Lesne wrote a book about overweight kids based on the things she observed in her own classroom. She noticed that teachers tend to be less demanding of overweight students. They might not even realize they're doing it, she observed, but teachers tend to ask these students fewer questions, and seem to pay less attention to them, as if they were trying to overlook them so as not to humiliate them in front of their classmates. It's a way of being protective, but by treating them this way—by making sure they avoid all competition—these teachers are just further handicapping the students. If you want to break this vicious cycle, you need to make some effort, too. If you know the answer to a question—or you want to be the captain in gym class who picks the teams—then raise your hand and speak up. Don't worry about standing out in front of everyone. Go for it! It's a sure way not to be left out.

i don't look
the part

While drama is not a team sport, it can certainly feel just as competitive. "In ninth grade," explains Alexandra, "we put on a play and a couple of us were auditioning for the same part. I wanted to go for the female lead. I really thought I was good for the part. But when it came to choosing the cast for the last play of the year, a slim girl was chosen instead of me. No one thought the resident fat girl could ever play the part of a pretty woman. As a consolation, the teacher suggested that I do my own comic monologue during intermission, based on something that I'd put together recently, but I really wasn't interested."

Alexandra suffered the painful experience of not being chosen. But she also knowingly chose an activity (theater in her case, but the same is true of things like dance and choir) where she is exposed to the opinions and judgments of others. She knows all too well that being a stereotype makes her life more difficult and she faces more cruelty because she doesn't conform to conventional ideas of what "the ideal" body type is. Despite all that, and despite the blow to her ego, Alexandra took it in stride. She loves drama so much that a setback like that didn't permanently affect her. She got straight into the production of another play, convinced that this time her talents would be appreciated, despite her looks.

She could have chosen to say yes to the monologue—she would've made use of her talent and shown the teachers that she was a team player who was willing to be a part of the production, even if it wasn't in her dream role. But if that was the third or fourth time this had happened to her, it was probably a wise choice to turn it down and explain to the teacher in charge of casting that she doesn't deserve to be pigeon-holed into being just "the funny one." She wants to be able to portray a full range of characters and not just those that narrow-minded teachers think a "girl like her" should play. So, where does she get this strength? Alexandra's passion fuels her desire to persevere, and to not give up when the going gets tough. It's certainly a good example to follow.

life of the party

For a long time, thirteen-year-old Louis hasn't really felt like he fit in with the group of people his age in his town. But one day he discovered that he really liked to dance. And it was dancing, and his love of hip-hop music, that helped him to turn things around. He was always invited over to his friends' houses to hang out on rainy days, or when the guys were just getting together to play video games. But when it came to getting together with girls, meeting at the mall, and things like that, he always seemed to be left out of the loop. Later on, the guys would spend hours telling him who said this and who did that. It was obvious to Louis that when his friends were trying to talk to girls, they just didn't want to be associated with him and his spare-tire gut.

One day, there was talk of organizing a dance at a nearby community center. Louis decided to take matters into his own hands and offered to be the DJ for the night. It was a really smart move and all his friends were speechless when they saw how much he knew about music.

Louis took a huge risk by deciding to go to the dance. He knew that many girls who he didn't know very well would be there. He broke out in a cold sweat just thinking about it. But as soon as he got there, his love of dancing and music got the better of him, and he really surprised everyone. Because he was so passionate about it, and because he did what he really wanted to, his enthusiasm allowed him to come out as the life of the party. The focus switched from his appearance to his talent and personality. And apparently, that impressed more than a few of the girls.

mall
rats

It only takes a few little rolls of flab to make life more difficult
and to find that you're being left out of activities with your friends.
Especially if you're a girl. And especially if that activity is shopping.

Helen is a fourteen-year-old clothes freak. Obviously she was looking forward to it when a bunch of her friends decided to meet up at the
mall. She tried on a slinky little dress and came out of the dressing room
with a big smile on her face, which quickly faded when she saw the reac-
tion from her friends. "I don't really think you can get away with that,"
said Rebecca. "Too many bulges." Meanwhile, her friends Beth and
Courtney emerged wearing microscopic short shorts, laughing loudly,
and sauntering down the corridor like it was a catwalk.

But Helen wasn't going to let it get to her. She told them, "Well, if
you think this dress doesn't look good on me, help me find one that
does!" So her friends made another lap around the store and came back
with armfuls of great outfits that were totally flattering on her.

Wearing clothes is not just about keeping covered up; it's about choosing how to display your body to others. It's now more acceptable to show a little flesh, even if you're not a perfect size six. Still, you might think the best thing to do is to keep covered up in oversized T-shirts and baggy pants. But actually, for girls, clothes that are fitted tend to be more flattering. So, try a bunch of different stores and styles before you tell yourself you can't wear trendy clothes because of your size. No matter how you decide to dress, the important thing is not to think that your less-than-perfect body is an enemy. Caring about your appearance, and caring about what you wear (and this is also true for guys) is important to everyone. Sometimes not caring about your appearance can communicate to others that you are trying *not* to be noticed. When you make the effort to look your best, it shows that you think you deserve attention and respect. It's also a really good way to keep your spirits up while you're striving to drop those extra pounds.

being left out . . . or leaving
yourself out?

All day long you are reminded that you have a body. Most of the time, you would rather forget about it, or punish it for being there. It's only natural that after a certain number of bad experiences, you would try to protect yourself and avoid putting yourself in the line of fire. Like, by turning down an invitation to a party, even though you're dying to go. Or not going to the pool with your friends because you don't want to be seen in a bathing suit. So, eventually, people stop asking you because you never say yes to anything. It's a trap that gradually distances you from your friends and their lives. The way to avoid this is to be true to yourself and to not lose sight of the things you really enjoy doing.

Being as brave as Helen, Louis, and Alexandra, who aren't afraid to put themselves out there, means subjecting yourself to the opinions of others. Even if you don't want to get up on an actual stage, try to break out of your shell. It's hard, of course, because you've become super-sensitive. It's painful to be judged by others when you know that they don't see you as you'd like to be seen. But all teenagers feel this way at some point. No teenage boy or girl can escape from feeling insecure about something. Don't let your weight keep you from enjoying all that life has to offer. In reality, most people aren't constantly making fun of you. A large part of it may well be in your imagination.

impossible

Whether you've got ten or twenty or thirty extra pounds, it feels just as bad to be discriminated against because of your weight. Striving to attain fashionable thinness is the same everywhere. All you have to do is flip through a fashion magazine and you'll be assaulted by an army of waify, twig-like women, and a bunch of well-built, fat-free men.

So, it's no wonder that you equate happiness and feeling good about yourself with having abs of steel. But let's get real. Models spend all of their time cultivating their bodies to look good on camera and in

standards

designer clothes. Many of them, especially the women, often put their health at risk by following ridiculous diets just to stay slim. Those dangerously skinny top models, some of whom subsist mainly on coffee, cigarettes, and drugs, are not as enviable as they may seem. If you need a role model, look around you and see which boys or girls are the most comfortable with themselves and their bodies: they are not necessarily the ones who are painfully thin.

the feminine

"Curves" is the word often used as a nice way of describing all those fuller parts of your body that you can't stand. But it also refers to the way women's bodies fill out during adolescence—the feminine figure formed by soft, round breasts and hips.

If you're a girl who, by the age of ten or eleven, is already a bit on the plump side, you will probably begin developing a bit sooner than the other girls your age. That's because reaching a certain weight is a trigger that tells your body it's time to start going through puberty. By the time you're in sixth or seventh grade, your breasts may begin to grow, even though many of the other girls in your class still look much younger. As a result, you might notice guys paying more attention to you—especially to certain parts of you—which can be surprising and exciting, but also uncomfortable. Your body has slowly, and sneakily, become the body of a woman, with all the sexuality that implies.

For many, it's hard to come to terms with these changes. You used to hate your double chin that stuck out from underneath your turtleneck, and now you've got to contend with

ideal

breasts and hips, which are also poking out of everything you own. Under these circumstances, it's hard to be thrilled about growing up. You might even prefer to hide the fact altogether by wearing unisex sweatsuits, or nothing but baggy jeans, or banishing from your closet anything that resembles a dress or a skirt. You might insult anyone "girly," and spend all your time hanging out with guys. That's one way to deal with it. Other girls go in a different direction and wear low-cut tops and skirts that are too tight or too short in order to attract the attention of any guy who might be looking. No matter what, developing before everyone else is not easy. If you started filling out around age twelve or thirteen, then you were probably pretty much in sync with your classmates who were buying bras at the same time. That way it's much simpler—at least you're all in it together. But of course, neither way is a

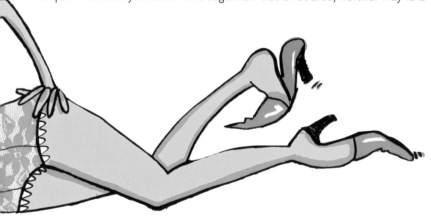

complete walk in the park. It might seem like even the girls who've got totally flat chests still get all of the guys just because they're skinny. Naturally, feeling less attractive than the others doesn't help you to feel good about your changing body. Some days, just being a girl is tough.

All of this is understandable. Establishing your identity as a woman is a task that lasts a lifetime (even though it won't always feel quite this difficult). The changes that occur during the teenage years are harder to accept if your body feels too large. You may wish you could hit rewind and go back to a time when you didn't have all this anxiety. In order to come to terms with your body, you need to distinguish between the curves that you have some control over—like large thighs, a double chin, and flabby arms that don't fit into skinny tops—and those that are part of being a woman—like breasts and wide hips. Being completely rock-hard without an ounce of fat isn't natural or healthy for a woman and, believe it or not, most guys don't think it's all that attractive either.

not man enough

Boys, like girls, also have to deal with gender roles from a young age. In defining your masculinity, physical strength is key—running fast, jumping high, throwing far. All of these things are very important to the male ego. The kind of teasing you get when you refuse to take a

turn on the rope swing at the lake or strike out in (another) baseball game is pretty sexist—comments like "You're such a girl," right?

In order to compensate for feeling not good enough athletically compared to the other boys, you might have learned to become the joker of the group. That way, despite your shortcomings, everyone would still want you around because you made them laugh. So, you got really good at coming up with quick comeback lines and producing really disgusting bodily noises that sent the girls running. It all helped solidify your place as one of the guys—and not one of the girls.

If that's the path you took, things have probably been working out pretty well up till now, right? Doctors have observed that most over-weight boys aren't motivated to take the weight off until they hit about thirteen or fourteen, even in cases of extreme obesity. This is the age when things get a little more complicated.

When you get to be a teenager, you're no longer so interested in avoiding girls at all costs. It even becomes interesting to hang around them and to be noticed by them. And that's the hard part—getting absolutely no response when you go and say hi to the girls. When other guys—the good-looking ones—say hi, the girls smile coyly. But with your extra pounds, it probably feels like the girls look right through you. It's a lot easier to be comfortable with your sexual identity when you get recognition from the opposite sex. Obviously, you can't force the girls to like you. But if you show an interest in them and you're nice to be around, you might be surprised by the results. And often, friendships develop into something more.

what about
romance?

Finding your place in a group of friends or classmates is important; so is feeling good about yourself. But there's more to life than just that. There's also romance—dating, hooking up, getting a boyfriend or girlfriend—whatever you want to call it. And right around now, that could be making you feel even more left out. But just because you're overweight it doesn't mean that no one will ever fall in love with you. No way!

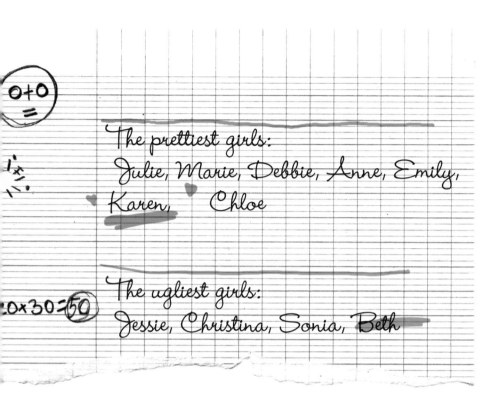

The prettiest girls:
Julie, Marie, Debbie, Anne, Emily, Karen, Chloe

The ugliest girls:
Jessie, Christina, Sonia, Beth

Between the ages of twelve and fourteen, love and sex play a major role in your daydreams. But, no matter how hard your friends try to make you believe otherwise, all the action is going on mainly in everyone's heads. Before embarking on real romance, everyone imagines how it could happen, sort of like a rehearsal. It's a way of practicing how to have a relationship before you actually do it. It's completely normal, and there'll be plenty of time later on for the real thing. One downside to all this fantasizing is that, because this is happening in your head and in your dreams, the picture you're envisioning tends to be a little more perfect than realistic. Ask any boy how he imagines the perfect girl, or ask any girl what her idea of the perfect guy is. The answer probably sounds a lot like a description of a popular actor or rock star, and nothing like any real live boy or girl at your school.

So, you don't look anything like the perfect boy or girl? Well, it doesn't mean that no one will ever love you or find you attractive. Some people insist that they'll only ever go out with a girl that looks just like Britney Spears, or with a guy as good looking as Johnny Depp. But that's not reality. When you fall in love, the object of your affection is rarely exactly like the perfect ideal you have in your head—even if you were to go out with Johnny Depp himself! Actually, it's often the little "flaws" and differences in a person that make them so loveable. So, don't worry about not being perfect—or even close to it. You never know what little thing will make someone fall in love with you, or you with them. A thin waist or bulging biceps are not enough to make a person fall in love. Likewise, when someone is truly in love, a few extra pounds would never change their mind.

your family pretends
not to see

Life at school is not always easy, especially when you're feeling down. It can be a real relief to go home, far from the criticism and back-stabbing of your alleged friends.

Do you have the kind of parents who rarely make any comments about your weight? It's great to have a safe haven like that. Of course, they're not blind—they see the same body that the kids at school do. But it may be that in your family, it's more acceptable to have put on a little weight. Pediatricians have noticed that some parents feign ignorance if they raise concerns about the child's weight gain: "What, my child needs to lose weight? I hadn't noticed!" This can be the case both in families where everyone is overweight and where only one person is.

"At least when I'm with my family, no one thinks I'm fat," says Elizabeth. "Which is good because, in a way, it helps me to think about other things. Last weekend, I got a second helping of dessert without even asking. And Mom is happy because she says that at least I like her cooking! Not like my skinny sister who just pushes the food around on her plate." Even though maintaining a proper weight is good for you, there are still many families who feel that a few extra pounds are a sign of a good appetite and therefore of good health. They don't think it's such a problem to be on the plump side.

Grandparents are sort of a wild card. Usually they've got lots of unconditional love to pass around, but then they also come out with comments like "Charlie, he's a stocky one!" which makes it hard to enjoy visits to their house—or grandma's famous chocolate layer cake.

Brothers and sisters are usually less tolerant; in fact, they can be downright brutal. If you're lucky enough to have one or two of these charming specimens in your family, then you are probably used to the same kind of jeers from them as you get from classmates. But at least at home, it's easier to fight back. If your sister says "Hey, nice love handles," you know her well enough to tell her to get out of your face. You can throw out a comeback without any hesitation and without letting it get you down— bickering is what siblings do best, right?

no one takes me
seriously

In such a laid-back atmosphere, you might sometimes wonder if your parents have even the slightest bit of concern for you. How can they ignore what seems so blatantly obvious to everyone else? Are they also pretending not to know what you go through at school? Deep down,

you might think that they still know everything that you're feeling, that they can read your thoughts, like they did when you were little.

But you need to be realistic. Your parents are only human and they can't always know what you don't tell them. By never saying anything, you're setting yourself up for misunderstandings that can turn into arguments. "Sometimes my father calls me a butterball, just as a joke," says Olivia. "It was funny when I was little, but he doesn't realize that now I'm really self-conscious about my weight and it hurts my feelings.

One day at school, I got called a lot of names and when I got home, he greeted me with that nickname and I just exploded. He didn't get it. But it had to come to a boiling point before I could explain to him the kind of things I put up with at school."

Before you explode and take it all out on your parents, remember that they love you just the way you are. They see you as their beautiful, precious child, their pride and joy, and may not realize that you could be sensitive about your appearance. Also, watching their own children turn into teenagers is difficult for them. Sometimes they tend to treat you like you're younger than you really are. When a father calls his thirteen-year-old daughter a butterball, he doesn't even realize that he's being insensitive; in fact, he would never think she's unhappy because she doesn't feel attractive.

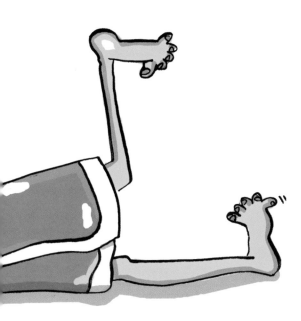

This drives you crazy, of course. But have you tried talking to them about it? No one's saying it'll be easy. You don't really want to admit to your parents that you have to endure teasing and rejection by your friends. And perhaps your parents are trying to respect your privacy and not butt into your life. You don't have to tell them every single little detail. But take the initiative and tell them how you feel. If you feel bad about yourself and you can't stand it anymore—tell them how serious it is. By expressing yourself this way, you're showing your parents that you are a responsible, articulate, self-aware person, and they're going to have to take you seriously.

your family never lets
you forget

On the complete other side of the coin, you might have the sort of parents who are always telling you to watch what you eat, especially at mealtimes. The kind who glare at you if you come home with a candy bar in your hand. Or it could be even worse: Your nutritionally-obsessed mother made you lose five pounds by putting you on a low-fat diet and then proudly announced your weight to all her friends. Now that's embarrassment. Other parents get obsessed with sports. "My mother is forever trying to get me to sign up for some athletic activity or another," says Nat. "And she always says 'You'll see, it will make you thinner'. And the minute she says that, it makes me want to grab a bag of potato chips and plop on the couch in front of the TV. Even my father is getting into it. Last Sunday, at breakfast, he started in on me with his two favorites: 'Eat some fruit, it's healthier' and 'What do you say to a quick jog in the park?'"

This kind of thing can really make you resent your parents for always being on your case and making you feel even worse than you already do. At least try to understand that if your parents are concerned about your weight, it's because they're concerned about you. Are they very conscious of their own weights? Did they have problems when they were your age because of their size? If so, it could explain why they won't leave you alone—because they don't want you to go through the same troubles that they did. You might find they have a lot more understanding for your situation than you thought.

A Healthy Diet

making your own
decisions

Parents who try to help out are the ones who understand the problem and take it seriously. But sometimes they tend to overdo it. They worry about everything you put in your mouth, look at you from every angle when you're in your bathing suit, sign you up for "slimming" activities, and organize your schedule like when you were six years old. They want to help, but they go about it without consulting you first, as if you were a helpless baby with no say in the matter.

So, you resist or you take an extra-large second handful of M&Ms when your mother tells you to take it easy. Going against your parents' advice is a completely normal defense mechanism. If they would just back off a little, you might think about what you need to do to lose a few pounds. As hard as it is, you have to tell them to give you some space. Let them know that you're glad you can count on them for support when you decide to tackle your weight issue. (You'll really need it then.) But for whatever reason, right now it's making things worse. Making the decision to change can only come from you.

So, while we're at it, some introspection might be in order. No matter how your parents deal with your weight, it probably bugs you. If they say nothing, you feel unloved. If they get too involved, you feel completely invaded. What's the perfect balance? You want your parents to help and support you, but without treating you like a child. The best way to bring that about is to learn about weight, health, and nutrition yourself. You need a better understanding of how you became overweight before you can fix it.

Cake

Potato chips

Candy bars

Popcorn

Candy

Ice cream

Pizza

Butter

Chocolate

Donuts

French fries

Mashed
potatoes

Cookies

Jam

Sugar

Milkshakes

a weighty past

A THOUSAND
TEMPTATIONS

HOW I GOT
TO BE
SO HEAVY

the body
mass index

it's not fair

the body mass index

𝒶 𝓇𝑒𝒸𝑒𝓃𝓉 𝓈𝓉𝓊𝒹𝓎 𝑜𝒻 𝓉𝑒𝑒𝓃𝒶𝑔𝑒 𝑔𝒾𝓇𝓁𝓈 found that 59 percent were dissatisfied with their bodies and 66 percent wanted to lose weight. Another survey found that about 50 percent of teenage boys also want to tone up. A portion of these teens have serious weight problems, but for others, it's simply a case of poor body image. So which side do you fall on? If everyone (doctors, teachers, parents, friends) has told you that you're overweight, there's probably some truth in it. But for others the answer is less obvious. Everyone may be saying that you look "just fine the way you are," even though you feel pudgy or plump. Who's right?

To figure it out, calculate your Body Mass Index (or BMI), a tool created by the World Health Organization and used by doctors to determine

whether a patient is over- or underweight. Here's the formula: Take the number of pounds you weigh and divide it by the number of inches tall you are. Once you get that answer, divide it by the number of inches tall you are again. Then take that answer and multiply it by the number 703.

So, for example, if you weigh 100 pounds and you're 5 feet (or 60 inches) tall, the calculation would go like this:

100 / 60 = 1.666

1.666 / 60 = .027

.027 x 703 = 19.527

So, your BMI would be about 19.5.

This number gives you an idea of the overall proportion of fat on your body. There isn't one ideal BMI for everyone because it varies by age and by sex, but the following chart shows the averages for various ages:

	BOYS	GIRLS
AGE	BMI	
ten-year-olds	16-17	17
twelve-year-olds	17-18	18
fourteen-year-olds	19	19-20

So if you're a twelve-year-old girl with a BMI of 19.5, as in the example above, your doctor might tell you that you have a slightly higher body mass than the average girl your age, but you're not overweight. The next chart shows what BMI is considered overweight for boys and girls at various ages:

	BOYS ♂	GIRLS ♀
AGE	BMI	
ten-year-olds	22	23
twelve-year-olds	24	25
fourteen-year-olds	26	27

the differences between
boys and girls

When you calculated your BMI, did you find out that it's right where it's supposed to be—but you still feel fat? If that's the case, chances are you're a girl. Boys generally have a much better body image than girls do. If they feel fat, then there's usually a good reason. Girls, on the other hand, tend to see themselves as being heavier than they really are. It may not be your weight that's causing your self-esteem problem, but something else—possibly the changes in your body that come along with puberty.

A quick biology lesson: Between the ages of ten and fifteen, girls gain on average about forty-five pounds, consisting of twenty pounds of fatty tissue and twenty-five pounds of muscle mass. Boys, during the same stage of development, gain about fifty-five pounds, of which only six pounds is fatty tissue and the remaining forty-nine pounds are muscle mass. Before puberty, body fat tends to accumulate in the lower parts of children's bodies, and this stays the same for girls after puberty. For boys, it's the opposite: They lose almost all fat below the waist.

Girls naturally produce more fatty tissue than boys. Obviously, this doesn't mean that all girls are overweight. The fat is distributed throughout a woman's entire body, and is necessary for her body to look and function the way it's supposed to. For example, look at a boy's legs: There are bones, muscle, and not much else. On a girl—even a thin girl—the leg is softer and more shapely. It's made up of bones, muscle, and also a decent amount of fat. At puberty, female hormones signal the body to prepare itself for a future pregnancy by stocking up fatty tissue to protect a baby. If a woman loses an unhealthy amount of weight, she will stop having her period—which means she can't get pregnant. The body knows it can't support a baby without a certain amount of fat. Naturally you lose some fat when you diet and work out, but you can't get rid of all of it completely. Everybody (including boys) needs some fat in order to live.

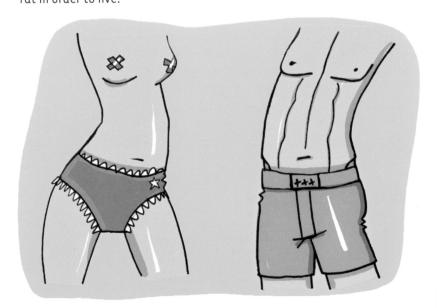

a weighty past

Say your dad, mom, grandpa, and aunt are all overweight. Does that mean that you'll be just like them and there's nothing you can do about it? If you come from a family where no one is exactly stick thin, you might feel like it's not even worth trying to fight your genes. Surely you've seen one of those news shows on TV that says that weight gain can be inherited from your parents. But the truth is that doctors believe genetics is only one small factor in the equation that determines how heavy a person turns out to be. There isn't a gene that causes someone to gain weight regardless of what they put in their mouth, except in very rare cases of serious illness. It is true that some people are more predisposed to weight gain than others because of their genes. However, those genes will only lead to weight gain if given the opportunity. In other words: If you have the genetic tendency to gain weight, and you eat more food than your body burns off through everyday movement and exercise, you will put on weight. Of course, it's entirely possible that everyone else in your family is thin and you are the only one who's chubby—even people who don't have overweight families can still get fat.

Don't glare at your chubby relatives too harshly. Scientists believe that the genes that predispose people toward weight gain are very common and have been around for generations. The ability to accumulate

At the beach, 1998

fatty tissue when food is plentiful was very useful to our ancestors. It allowed those who had this gene to fare better in times of famine (their bodies could burn the extra fat they'd saved up to produce energy when there wasn't enough food to do the job), allowing them to survive. So, basically, these "good" genes have been handed down through the years . . . all the way to you.

Canadian scientists were able to observe this tendency by studying the large number of obese children (practically 70 percent) in the Inuit population of Alaska. Up until very recently, they had very little food to eat each winter. Only those who could keep some weight on were able to survive the long periods of famine. They gained weight when there was food, and then burned it off each year when the food ran out. But as soon as they were able to increase their food supply and ensure a stable amount all year long, there was no famine period to burn off the excess fat, and their bodies' ability to pack it on made them overweight.

it's not fair

If you seem to put on weight more easily than others even though you eat the same amount, it means that your metabolism is slow, most likely for genetic reasons.

There are some lucky people who can eat whatever they want and never get fat. Even when they're just resting, their bodies expend a lot of energy to maintain

a normal temperature of 98.6 degrees and to breathe, digest, and perform all the bodily functions that allow them to live. They are naturally thin and they can eat more than other people because they burn the energy acquired and don't store the rest as fat.

This genetic inequality demonstrates what nutritional researchers have been claiming for years: Not all fat people eat more than thin people. In each category, there are heavy eaters and light eaters, those who like food and those who don't. Only about 15 percent of overweight teenagers are genuine overeaters. The majority (85 percent) eat about the same as thin teenagers. The difference between a thin person and an overweight person who eat a similar amount of food could be genetics, it could be the amount of physical activity each one gets, or it could be a combination of both.

Don't take this as a signal to head for the fridge because there's no hope! If you have put on weight, it is because you have eaten more than your body can burn. It's not fair, but to get and stay thin, you're going to have to work harder than most and be more careful about what you eat.

a thousand temptations

"Watch what you eat!" You can't get the phrase out of your head, right? Well it's a lot easier said than done. Actually, what you really need to do is not watch. It's hard not to see the ice cream in the freezer or kitchen cupboards full of potato chips. In our society, food is abundant and on display. When you were a kid, your parents pretty much decided what you did and didn't eat. But now that you're older, they're not solely responsible for picking all your meals. You have much more independence and choice over what you put in your mouth. And many of those extra pounds might be a result of that independence in a world full of temptations.

You know all too well that to stay slim, you must not eat more than you need. Say it that way and it sounds simple. But if you've been eating poorly for a while now, your body doesn't always give you the right signals for how much it needs. If one day you eat less than you normally do, you get hunger pangs. On the other hand, you're capable of eating much more than your body needs before you get to the point where you feel so full that you can't put another thing in your mouth.

Wild animals use internal signals to regulate their body weight and are able to maintain the correct weight as long as the food supply is adequate. This is why they never get fat. A wild cat will catch a mouse when it's hungry and then wait until hunger returns before eating again. If he ate a big mouse, he might wait a bit longer than normal before catching another. Cats that are house pets, on the other hand, are well-fed by their owners and, as a result of eating several helpings of cat food a day, can become overweight, just like humans.

If you pay attention, your body will give you a good idea of when you've eaten enough. But a lot of the time, we don't listen to what our

bodies tell us. We eat when it's dinnertime, or when it's lunchtime, or when a friend offers us a snack, even if we're not hungry yet. For humans, eating is not just about filling up the belly. It's a way of socializing, a way of enjoying the company of others. It's part of the way humans relate to one another. (You wouldn't have a birthday party without cake, right?) So we eat whether our bodies need food or not, as long as the atmosphere is right, or the food is appetizing.

the choice is yours

It's easy to overeat when food tastes good, and even easier when there is a large selection available.

Think about the last party you went to. By the time you finished with the appetizers, you were hardly hungry anymore. If more of the same kind of food was put in front of you, you might have turned it down. But when the main course was served, with a different smell and taste and texture, your eyes lit up. By the time dessert came around, even though two minutes before you swore you couldn't eat another thing, the sight of something new and sweet revived your appetite.

The more variety that is presented during the course of a meal—or during the course of the day—the more we are likely to eat. It's not known for sure what controls this reflex, but it seems that our brains set the empty/full indicator back to zero when a new kind of food becomes available. This is true of animals in captivity, too. Laboratory mice maintain a stable weight if they're fed a steady diet of corn. But if they get a smorgasbord of variety—cheese, dried fruit, sugar, cookies—and if the menu changes daily to mix it up, they triple in size. They just snack and snack . . . remind you of anyone?

snack foods can be
dangerous

You don't need to be at a party to overeat. Maybe you eat a donut on the way to school because you don't have time for a real breakfast, and a candy bar at break time. Maybe you have a bag of potato chips on the way to soccer practice and make a trip to the fridge before dinner. And don't forget a soda to wash it all down. You finish the list.

If you usually eat healthy-sized portions of nutritious foods during meals, in-between-meal snacking might be your problem. Many people only remember what they ate for breakfast, lunch, and dinner, and don't even realize how much they're eating in between.

While some dinner foods are certainly unhealthy, it's even more common for snack foods to have little nutritional value. That's because our favorite foods to snack on are those that are easy to eat and full of fat, sugar, or both—things like cheese puffs and candy bars. Unfortunately, we're also more likely to overeat these kinds of foods. (You don't usually throw down an entire bag of carrot sticks while watching TV at night, do you?) While eating too much of any food will make you gain weight, it's much easier to eat too much junk food than it is to eat too many vegetables. And consider this: You only have to eat about 5 percent more than your body needs everyday, for one year, to put on ten pounds of fat! The occasional treat, like going for ice cream after a good report card, is not going to have dire consequences. But making it a daily habit to snack on unhealthy foods will have long-term effects.

not enough
moving
around

You know that weight gain is caused by an imbalance between what goes in and what gets burned off. What goes in is very important, but even at an age when your body needs lots of energy to grow, burning off energy by being physically active is also very important. In other words, there are two things you'll need to do to lose weight: Eat smaller and healthier meals and snacks, and get more exercise. Exercise doesn't just mean working out in a gym for thirty minutes, or spending an hour a day in basketball practice. It also means all the little movements and activities we do each day, from walking up stairs to running to catch the bus. More teenagers today are overweight than in years

past, and many experts believe the difference is in the amount of exercise they get. People today don't move nearly as much as they used to. Central heating keeps us warm in the winter so we don't need to go chop wood before walking five miles through the snow to get to school. We don't have to get water from the well. And we don't have to spend all day doing the laundry by hand. We've got machines that do all this for us.

Obviously, everyone in an industrialized country benefits from progress. But if you've gotten a little plump, it's probably due in part to the fact that you're not moving enough.

You go to school by car or bus. If you live in an apartment, you take an elevator to get to your floor. And when you get home, you watch a little bit of TV before doing your homework. Then you go to bed. Not much opportunity there for your body to burn off extra energy.

To be physically active, you don't necessarily have to be athletic. Sports are a great way to keep fit, burn off steam, and get in shape. But any activity in which you participate intensely at least three times a week will have a real impact. To burn off two pounds of fat, you need to swim for seventeen hours, ride a bike for thirty hours or walk for sixty-three hours. Of course, you don't have to do all of this straight in one day! Because you're doing it over time, you can expect to safely lose about one to two pounds a week if you consistently eat less food and get more exercise.

The essential thing is to exercise regularly—this will make all the difference. So run up the stairs, ride your bike to your friend's house, walk or swim on weekends, and rollerblade or shoot hoops before you do your homework every day. It's true: Playing outside is just as important as doing school work!

Let's get back to your eating habits for a minute. Now you know that it's easier to overeat junk food than healthy food, and that sometimes you eat just because food is there, not because you're truly hungry. But there's also another reason why it's hard to avoid the fridge sometimes—we find comfort in food.

Puberty is a time of soul-searching. Teenagers have a lot of anxiety since there's so much going on in their lives. One way to feel better when the going gets tough is to indulge in something delicious. A case of the blues, a fight with your best friend or your parents, a math test that you're worried about—any of these events can bring on an uncontrollable craving for an ice cream sundae or a big fat salami sandwich. From the moment we're born, food is a source of comfort. For the newborn baby, hunger and separation from Mommy are the main sources of suffering. And, as if by magic, when the baby cries, he gets milk and someone to hold him while he drinks it. We all share this memory of having been satisfied by a full belly in the arms of our mothers. The memory stays in our subconscious, and food stays connected with comfort. So, when you're feeling down, you grab something to eat! And when you feel like eating to calm your emotions, it's not a boneless, skinless chicken breast or green vegetables that you crave—you want something sweet that

reminds you of childhood, when everything was happy and easy. Some people have the urge to eat more strongly than others do when they're feeling down. Why? Because that's their personality. If you're one of them, you'll probably always have these urges, but if you become aware of them now, you can learn to control them. The best way is to either resolve the situation that's troubling you or, if that's not possible, to distract yourself. So if you crave a candy bar after a fight with your sister, first try and talk it out with her and see if you can reach a compromise. No luck? Take a long walk instead of heading straight for the kitchen. You'll clear your mind and avoid eating food your body doesn't really need.

don't sweat the
big stuff

Of course, not every problem can be solved with a quick talk or a run around the block. If something really serious happens, like your parents decide to get a divorce or someone you care about dies, you might find yourself craving food even more, and for a longer period of time.

It's the same underlying process: You're seeking comfort in food. But it also might be a way of telling your family that you need help deal-

ing with whatever's going on. Under these circumstances, putting on weight might be a silent way of saying, "Please pay attention to me, I'm not happy."

If this describes you, the first thing to do is find someone to talk to. If you can, confide in your parents. If that won't work, find people who can point you in the right direction—a friend, a relative, a guidance counselor, or a teacher at school. When the problems have subsided, then you can think about losing weight. It will work better if you resolve the issues before trying to take off the pounds.

who can help?

GET MOVING!

the rules

talk to
your friends

HOW TO
LOSE WEIGHT

how to deal with cravings

it worked! now what?

getting
help

So, you've decided to do something about your weight.
Maybe you've tried before. You've given up hot dogs and burgers and taken the
puppy out for a jog on Sunday mornings. That's a great way to start, but if you
want to go all the way, you've got to stick with it. To do that, you might want to
ask for help, especially if you've got more than a couple pounds to lose.

Since your parents are in charge of grocery shopping and meal planning,
they need to be in on your project. Family meals might be part of the problem.
If you're not going to become a chef or earn a degree in nutrition studies in the
next few months, the best thing to do is to see a dietitian. This is someone who
will analyze your eating habits and show you how to improve them, which is
vital if you want to make changes.

Did your parents offer to make an appointment with a health professional
the minute you talked to them about your problems? Are they willing to go with
you to the first appointment? Are they going to support you and change some
of their habits, too? If this is the case, you have great parents! Take advantage and make use of their help.

Your family doctor will help you to analyze your weight issues and carry out tests to make sure that your weight isn't caused by an illness. After she has checked you out, she can refer you to a dietitian.

A dietitian is not a doctor. He or she is a person with special training in nutrition who will help you to formulate a plan that you can stick to every day to help you eat better and lose weight.

what if they
don't help?

𝒩ot all parents think it's important to call in the health professionals. They think it's their job to know what's best to feed their children, and they're not necessarily going to be thrilled to hear your thoughts on the food they serve. As you may have already noticed, some adults are not willing to question their ways and to make changes in their habits. If that sounds like your parents, you're going to have to find ways to convince them this is important.

Maybe your parents do know a thing or two about nutrition, and try to serve healthy meals. They might tell you that it couldn't be the food they prepare

Hey, can I have some more candy?

that's making you fat, especially if you're the only one in the family putting on weight. They could be right, but then again, maybe their cooking is just fine for everyone else in the house, but you need them to make some changes to help you lose weight. Hefty servings of lasagna may be OK for your dad who's really tall and has a physically demanding job, but you're just an average teenager who has to spend a lot of time sitting in classrooms. If you think lighter dinners would help you meet your goals, try to explain that to your parents.

The stickiest of situations is probably when everyone in your family is a bit on the plump side, but they're all fine with it. They don't get bent out of shape over the buttered pancakes and bacon Mom serves every morning. In this case, it's harder to bring up the subject because your decision to lose weight might feel like a form of betrayal. Don't torture yourself. You don't have to be a carbon copy of everyone in your family. Even if your parents aren't interested in losing weight, let them know that your weight is making you unhappy and that you need their help. There may well be a huge gap between what you're served and what you need to eat to lose weight.

Another possibility: You have a family where everyone is obsessed with their weight, whether or not they need to be. It could be that your mother serves you smaller portions or makes you special meals based on a diet that she's on herself. But the right diet for an adult isn't necessarily the right diet for a young person. It may even be that because she's limiting your portions, you get hungry between meals and are more tempted to snack. Tell her you've read that diets, like prescription medications, need to be tailored to individual needs, and that what works for an adult is not going to work for a teenager.

Is it serious, doc?

who can help?

There are several options. If you really are overweight (three to four points above the recommended BMI for your age), then you should make an appointment with your family doctor. He might send you for tests because there could be a medical reason why. Your weight can even cause medical problems, such as a condition called diabetes. If nothing is detected, he will give you some advice and possibly put you in touch with a dietitian.

The dietitian's job is to give you practical solutions and ways to alter your eating habits, perhaps by giving you some recipes or meal-planning suggestions and tips on how to grocery shop. This is why it's very useful to have the person who does the shopping come along, at least for the first appointment.

The dietitian will have you make a list of the things you eat during the week, and probably for the few weeks before your appointment. It is important to go along with it, without cheating and without leaving anything out. If you have a few of your friend's french fries at lunch, write it down. A few gulps of OJ straight from the carton—write it down. Nothing is too big or too small to include in your food diary. The dietitian will also ask your parents about what meals they serve and how they're prepared. He might ask some surprising questions, like "How long does a bottle of oil or a stick of butter last in your house?" This lets him know whether the family chef tends to go heavy or light on potentially fattening ingredients.

According to your tastes and your habits, the dietitian will teach you how to make good choices. You like croissants, but you also like English muffins. The English muffin has less fat, so it's the better choice. For the same reason, if you like to eat pasta, smother it in tomato sauce instead of butter and cheese.

Often, the dietitian will be able to spot easy ways to change the way food is prepared at your house to make it healthier. It may be that your dad is a bit heavy-handed with the butter when he coats a pan before cooking chicken breasts. In that case, it's just a matter of cutting back from three pats to one pat—something no one is likely to even notice, but which could help you lose weight.

Food Diary

Monday: Breakfast
yogurt, 2 donuts, 6 slices of buttered toast, a piece of candy, hot chocolate, orange juice

Lunch
can of soda, 2 hot dogs, fries, apple turnover, potato chips, candy bar

Dinner Strawberry milk, 3 slices of pizza, box of cookies, 20-ounce bottle of soda

not a diet, but a lifestyle
change

A dietitian will also give advice to suit the lifestyle habits of your family. Reassure your parents that he won't ask them to make you special meals or to use special ingredients that are expensive or hard to find.

Only in very extreme cases will a dietitian put you on an official "diet." You won't have a weekly menu that says exactly what you should eat. You probably won't even have to count calories.

This sort of dieting is not really followed anymore. Strict rules and regulations might allow you to lose weight initially, but as soon as your guard is down, you go back to your old ways and the weight creeps back on. The best solution is to change your habits gradually and for good. It's hard at first, and you will probably have some cravings for unhealthy foods that you know you should avoid most of the time. But if you hang in there, after about ten days, those desires to snack will begin to subside and it will get easier to resist. Why? Because your body will simply adjust to the changes. If you follow the dietitian's advice, your tastes will change and you will get used to eating differently. You will still enjoy food like you always did, but without putting on extra weight.

support and

Once the plan of attack has been decided, you will probably have a monthly appointment with the dietitian so he can monitor your progress. Don't miss these appointments, even if you feel like you've cheated (or even if you know you have!) He knows only too well just how hard it is to change habits and it's his job to help you. It may take as long as a year to lose all the weight you want. Even if everything is going smoothly, there will be

encouragement

times when your weight-loss levels off and you're no longer dropping pounds as quickly as before. Eating less tells your body that it's famine time, so it tries to hold on to its extra fat, just like the Inuits in Alaska during the winter. If you lost ten pounds over the course of a few months, your body is not as heavy as it used to be and so it burns less energy to get through the day. Therefore, it needs less food than it did before. To continue losing weight at this point, you'll need to keep your metabolism up by getting more physical activity.

Weight-loss takes time, and you may get discouraged at some point along the way. The dietitian's support will help you get through those moments. Once you've achieved your ideal weight and stayed there for a while, that's when the dietitian will leave you alone. His job is also to help you become independent and to teach you how to regulate your own weight without his regular assistance. After about a year, you should be practically ready to be a dietitian yourself with all the knowledge you'll have gained, and with any luck, you'll have the skills to stay fit permanently.

the rules

The dietitian will teach you about the basics of a healthy diet. The most important thing is to eat well at mealtimes. Your body is burning energy to help you grow into an adult, so it needs a sufficient amount of fuel at regular intervals. The best way to lose weight is to make sure you never get hungry between meals so that you are not tempted to eat unhealthy snacks. To do this, you need to eat enough to keep you going for a few hours. The way to do this is to eat foods that have nutrients like protein and fiber, which make you feel fuller, longer. Junk food tends to not have many nutrients, so very soon after you eat it, you feel hungry again. The first meal of the day is vital. The more you eat in the morning, the less likely you will be tempted to eat junk at eleven o'clock, or even for the rest of the day. Drink milk instead of soda, and eat whole-wheat toast and fruit instead of donuts or pastries, which are high in unhealthy types of fat and yet leave you feeling hungry in no time at all. Cereal is also a good option, but avoid the over-sweetened, sugary kinds (pretty much anything that is brightly colored or comes with a prize inside the box). They don't fill you up as well as whole-grain cereals and you have to eat a lot of them (and therefore a lot of sugar) to get through the morning.

For lunch at school, you can either bring a meal from home or eat in the cafeteria. Go for the salad bar if there is one. If not, a sandwich with a small amount of meat and loads of vegetables is a good choice. Whatever you do, don't skip it altogether. That will only send you running for the vending machine later in the day—and there usually aren't many healthy options there. Snacking when you get home is OK if you pick the right things: Try peanut but

ter on celery sticks, reduced-fat cheese with apple slices, or nonfat yogurt with crunchy whole-grain cereal stirred in.

This doesn't mean you have to deprive yourself of an outing to a fast-food joint every now and then—just don't make a habit of it. If you find yourself eating out often, look for the lighter choices on the menu. Chicken tenders can be just as bad as burgers because they're fried in flour and oil. Order a grilled chicken sandwich instead—hold the mayonnaise. Or opt for a salad, but make sure the dressing is low-fat. Stay away from the fries and have milk or water instead of a soda or shake and you'll be fine.

When you're eating out at restaurants, don't fill up on dinner rolls before you even get to the main course. Order baked or grilled meat instead of fried. Fresh fruit or sorbet is a better dessert option than cake or ice cream. While low-carb diets have been big in recent years, it's not a good idea to cut out carbohydrates altogether. Foods high in carbohydrates like pasta, bread, rice, and potatoes are needed in order for your body to produce energy. If you cut them out completely, your body will miss them, and you'll get strong cravings for chips and bread and sweets. The best thing to do is choose "good carbs." That means things like whole-wheat bread, brown rice, baked potatoes with the skin left on, and plenty of fruits and vegetables. Because these foods are less processed than white bread and potato chips, they contain more fiber, which is good for you and keeps you feeling full. As for drinks, you know that soda isn't a good idea, but things like fruit punch and lemonade can have a lot of sugar, too. The best choices are water, milk, and orange juice. Smoothies are a great way to get more fruit in your diet, but have them in place of a snack rather than in addition to your snack, and make sure they're made with whole fruit, low-fat milk, or yogurt and not a ton of sugar.

So what do you do if you're hungry in between meals? First, make sure it's your body that truly needs food and it's not just your mind that's bored or stressed. Then, satisfy your hunger with foods that are high in nutrients, not high in sugar. Have some string cheese, a yogurt, or some baby carrots.

Whole-grain foods that contain complex carbohydrates (rather than simple carbohydrates—otherwise known as sugar) are your best bet. They give you a lot of energy and keep you going for a long time because they take longer for your body to digest. Complex carbs can be found in things like pasta, bread, rice, and beans. Each of your meals should have some complex carb–rich foods in it.

how to deal with
cravings

You know that snacking often leads to overeating, but how can you break the habit? It's usually when you get home from school, before dinner, or after dinner that you lose your self-control, right? Cravings sometimes happen even when you've eaten enough at mealtimes. You're not really hungry . . . but you still want to eat something. Try to think about how you feel when this happens. Are you feeling lonely? Pick up the phone and call a friend. Are you worried, or tired? Take a bubble bath, or listen to some music. Are you bored? Take the dog for a walk, go for a bike ride, surf the Internet, or start an art project. Sometimes all you have to do is keep your hands busy with something else and the desire to snack goes away by itself.

Other times, you might get an overwhelming desire to eat a certain kind of food (chocolate, ice cream, hot dogs, whatever). It might seem like a good idea to completely cut that food out of your life. But that's not actually the best way to deal with it—denying yourself what you love most only makes you want it more. It's much better to still allow yourself the foods you like and just limit the amount. Instead of grabbing the box of cookies from the cupboard and sitting down in front of the TV with it, look at the nutrition label and see what the serving size is. If the box says one serving is two cookies, take out two cookies and put the box away. You'll naturally eat a lot less when you have to go all the way back to the kitchen to get more. The same goes for ice cream, cereal, tortilla chips, and everything else: Find out how much one serving is, measure it out, and put the container away.

talk to your
friends

At this point, you understand how to eat a balanced diet. Your parents have hopefully accepted the advice of the dietitian, they're doing everything they can to help you, and they're being supportive. You now need to get your friends on board.

Why? Because you spend a lot of time with them and they probably haven't made the decision, like you have, to eat more healthfully. They're still going to be eating a ton of junk food, and they're going to be offering you some. Instead of making up excuses every time, just tell them what's going on. Tell them that you've seen a specialist about your weight problem and you

want to pay better attention to what you eat. Worried that they'll make fun of

you? It's possible. A group of friends is kind of like a band, each one plays their

own part, but you're pretty much in sync with each other. When one member

goes off and does something different, it disturbs the group. No matter what

happens, hang in there. Remember that if you give in to a milkshake at the

diner one day and nachos while hanging out at the mall the next, pretty soon

you'll undo all the progress you've worked so hard for. After they've adjusted

to the new you, real friends will support you and not try to undermine your

efforts.

get moving!

Your friends can actually be a big help to you. You know that you have to get moving to burn off more energy and calories, but maybe sports aren't your thing. What if you signed up for a club or activity with a friend? Studies show that working out with a buddy really helps keep people motivated.

If you find yourself always trying to put off exercise, joining a gym is a great idea. At a health club, you'll have regular classes or training sessions, and when you write in "hip-hop aerobics class, 7 pm, Tuesday" on the calendar, you'll feel more obligated to actually show up. Plus, if you do it with a friend, you'll have even more reason to go—if you don't, you'll be letting her down! It's also great to have a buddy when you're a beginner at the activity you're doing, because you'll both be starting at the same level so you'll feel less self-conscious. Squash, swimming, dance, tennis, yoga, pilates, bike riding, boxing—it doesn't really matter what you do, as long as it gets you moving and you enjoy it.

If the thought of working out still makes you groan, think of ways to incorporate more activity into your daily life. If you live close enough to school and the roads are safe, why not walk or ride your bike there instead of taking the bus? You'll have to leave a little earlier, but you'll be totally awake and alert by the time you get there (instead of yawning through first period like usual).

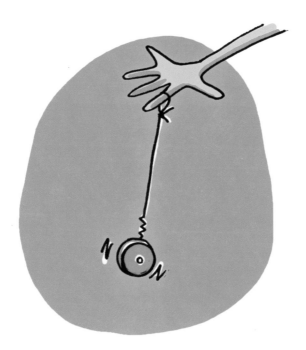

On the weekend, think of more active things to do instead of sitting in front of the TV. Go swimming with friends or get some fresh air on a hike. If your parents always say they should get more exercise, drag them along, too. Treat your little brother to a game of tag. Even doing laps around the mall counts. Give it some thought and try to get in at least five to six hours of exercise each week. Increasing your energy output is crucial to losing weight. Besides, being active helps you blow off steam and keeps your hand out of the cookie jar.

it worked!
now what?

Congratulations!

Your jeans are hanging down around your hips, when before you couldn't even pull them on! Even more than the number on the scale, this sort of thing is the best proof of the hard work you've just done.

At this point, you might be fantasizing about becoming the new class heartthrob, or about how awestruck all of your friends are going to be at your incredible transformation. Just so you're not disappointed, keep in mind that it might not turn out exactly like that. If you only had a few pounds to lose, chances are most people won't even notice the change. On the other hand, if your weight loss was significant, it will have taken you several months to accomplish. And because you're at an age when everyone is growing and changing at a rapid pace, your improvements—which seem glaringly obvious to you—might go unnoticed by everyone else.

So was it really worth it? You probably thought it would change your relationships, help you to fit in better, and have more friends. Was all that effort for nothing? Not at all. Your friends aren't going to suddenly open their eyes one day and see you differently. After shedding your hefty exterior, you'll still be the same person. But slowly, the way you feel about yourself will change. You'll gradually lose all those little hangups that made you hold back. The satisfaction of having succeeded, of getting rid of all that weight that was weighing you down, will make you more confident. You won't be constantly concerned about the size of your jeans. You'll be able to swim and dance and hang out with everyone else without feeling self-conscious.

A lot of the obstacles that made it hard for you to be yourself are now gone. But you've still got to do your part. It takes more than just being thin to have good friends. You have to be nice, sincere, open, generous, and interested in other people. All the qualities you want in a friend, you have to offer up in order to receive them back.

When you were preoccupied with your weight, you might not have had time to think about all that. But now you do, so go for it!

suggestions for further reading

Books

Overweight: A Handbook for Teens and Parents by Tania Heller, M.D.
(McFarland & Company, 2005)

The Can-Do Eating Plan for Overweight Kids and Teens: Helping Kids Control Weight, Look Better, and Feel Great by Michelle Daum, M.S., R.D., with Amy Lemley (Quill, 1997)

Teenage Fitness: Get Fit, Look Good, and Feel Great! by Kathy Kaehler (HarperResource, 2001)

Fueling the Teen Machine by Ellen Shanley and Colleen Thompson (Bull Publishing Company, 2001)

Toning for Teens: The 20-Minute Workout that Makes You Look Good and Feel Great! by Joyce L. Vedral (Warner Books, 2002)

Web sites

KidsHealth—Staying Healthy
www.kidshealth.org/kid/stay_healthy/
Articles on how to eat right and stay fit, plus a Body Mass Index (BMI) calculator.

Seventeen magazine—Health
www.seventeen.com/health
Workouts, recipes, quizzes, articles, and more.

index

A

acceptance from family about
    weight, 44, 83
activities for exercise, 71, 72, 74, 99
adolescence, impact on bodies,
    34–36, 39, 58–59
age and Body Mass Index (BMI),
    57–58, 85
amount of food vs. exercise,
    64, 71, 72
ancestors' survival, role of fat
    in, 61–62
animals, internal signals to
    regulate hunger, 66
appearance, caring about, 29–30

B

being left out. See left out (being)
BMI (Body Mass Index), 56–58, 85
body changes during adolescence,
    34–36, 58
body image, 56, 58–59

Body Mass Index (BMI), 56–58, 85
boys
    body image vs. girls, 58–59
    masculine ideal (body), 37–40
    "perfect," 41–42
breakfast, importance of, 90–91

C

carbohydrates, 93
causes of weight problems, 56–77
    age and Body Mass Index (BMI),
        57–58, 85
    ancestors' survival, role of fat
        in, 61–62
    body image, 56, 58–59
    Body Mass Index (BMI), 56–58, 85
    boys vs. girls, body image, 58–59
    comfort from food, 74–77
    diabetes, 85
    differences (body image) between
        boys and girls, 58–59

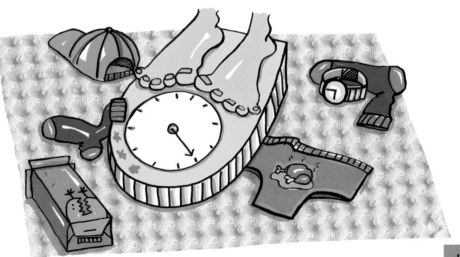

family eating habits, 18
famine, survival during, 61–62, 89
fat, importance of, 59, 61–62
   genetics as factor, 18, 60–62, 63
   girls vs. boys, body image, 58–59
   medical reasons, 85
   metabolism impact, 62–63, 90
   problems and weight gain, 74–77
   survival of ancestors, role of fat
     in, 61–62
   See also eating habits; exercise
cereals, healthy, 91
choices (food), making good, 86
clothes, shopping for, 28–30
comfort from food, 74–77
competition, avoiding, 22–23
complex carbohydrates, 93
covering up weight with clothes,
   29, 35
cravings, 88, 93, 94–95
"curves," 34, 36

D

daily life and exercise, 74, 99–100
dances, being left out of, 26–27
decisions about weight, making your
   own, 52–53
defending your weight, 17, 18–19,
   20, 45
desserts, healthy, 92
diabetes, 85
dieting caution, 88, 89. *See also*
   healthy diet rules
dietitian for help with losing weight,
   80–81, 85–87, 88, 90
diets, tailored to individual needs, 84
differences (body image) between
   boys and girls, 58–59
differences in people and
   romance, 42

discrimination about weight, 18–19,
   20, 23, 24, 25
doctor for help with losing weight,
   81, 85
drama (theater), being left out of,
   24–25
drinks, healthy, 91, 92, 93

E

eating habits, 64–70
   amount of food vs. exercise, 64,
     71, 72
   animals, internal signals to
     regulate hunger, 66
   choices (food), making good, 86
   comfort from food, 74–77
   cravings, 88, 93, 94–95
   dietitian for help with, 80–81,
     85–87, 88, 90
   family eating habits, 18
   hunger, regulated by internal
     signals, 66–67
   internal signals to regulate hunger,
     66–67
   junk food, danger of, 69–70, 74,
     75–76, 90, 92
   overeating, 63, 68–69, 70
   snack foods, danger of, 69–70, 74,
     75–76, 90, 92, 94
   socializing and eating, 67
   variety of foods and overeating,
     68–69, 74
   wild animals, internal signals to
     regulate hunger, 66
   See also causes of weight
     problems; exercise; healthy diet
     rules
eating out, healthy, 92–93
effort (making) to break cycle of
   being left out, 23

encouragement for losing weight, 80, 82–84, 88–90, 96–97, 102

exercise, 71–76
  activities for, 71, 72, 74, 99
  amount of food vs., 64, 71, 72
  daily life and, 74, 99–100
  friends' support for, 98–99
  industrialized countries and, 72
  metabolism impact, 62–63, 90
  regular activity, importance of, 74, 99–100
  See also causes of weight problems; eating habits

expectations (realistic) for losing weight, 101–103

F

family and overweight members, 44–53
  acceptance from family, 44, 83
  decisions about weight, making your own, 52–53
  defending your weight, 17, 18–19, 20, 45
  eating habits, 18
  grandparents, 45
  health and, 44, 50
  ignoring overweight issues, 44, 46
  obsessive parents, 50–52, 84
  parents, talking to about overweight issues, 46–49
  siblings and, 45
  support for losing weight, 80, 82–84
  talking to parents about overweight issues, 46–49
  unconditional love from family, 44, 45, 48

See also left out (being); overweight, under happy; standards (impossible)

famine, survival during, 61–62, 89

fantasies, romantic, 41–42

fast-food, 92

fat, importance of, 59, 61–62

"fat" label, 9, 13, 14

fattening ingredients in meals, 86

feelings about being overweight, 9, 56. *See also* overweight, under happy

feminine ideal (body), 24, 32, 34–36

fiber, 90

"flaws" in people and romance, 42

food. *See* eating habits; healthy diet rules

friends' support for losing weight, 96–99, 102

fruits, 91, 92, 93

G

genetics as factor of weight problems, 18, 60–62, 63

girls
  body image vs. boys, 58–59
  feminine ideal (body), 24, 32, 34–36
  "perfect," 41–42

grandparents and weight issues, 45

guilt feelings about being overweight, 18–19, 20

H

health and weight issues, 44, 50

healthy diet rules, 90–95
  breakfast, importance of, 90–91
  carbohydrates, 93
  cereals, 91

complex carbohydrates, 93
cravings, 88, 93, 94–95
desserts, 92
drinks, 91, 92, 93
eating out, 92–93
fast food, 92
fiber, 90
fruits, 91, 92, 93
low-carb diets, 92–93
lunch, 91–92
mealtimes, eating well at, 90,
    91–92
milk vs. soda, 91, 92, 93
portion sizes, 94
protein, 90
restaurants, 92–93
salads, 91, 92
sandwiches, 91, 92
serving sizes, 94
simple carbohydrates (sugar),
    avoiding, 91, 92, 93
smoothies, 93
snacking (healthy), 92, 93
vegetables, 93
whole-grains, 91, 93
See also eating habits; exercise;
    losing weight
help (professional) for losing weight,
    77, 80–81, 82, 85–86, 85–87,
    88, 90
humor, using to your advantage, 17,
    20, 38–39
hunger, regulated by internal signals,
    66–67

I

ignoring overweight issues by family,
    44, 46
impossible standards. See standards
    (impossible)

industrialized countries and
    exercise, 72
internal signals to regulate hunger,
    66–67

J

jokes about weight, 15–17, 18
journal of foods eaten, keeping, 86
judgments of others, subjecting
    yourself to, 24, 32
junk food, danger of, 69–70, 74,
    75–76, 90, 92

L

labels about weight, 9, 13–15
leaving yourself out vs. being left
    out, 31–32
left out (being), 22–27
    competition, avoiding, 22–23
    dances, being left out of, 26–27
    drama (theater), being left out of,
        24–25
    effort (making) to break cycle, 23
    judgments of others, subjecting
        yourself to, 24, 32
    leaving yourself out vs., 31–32
    opinions of others, subjecting
        yourself to, 24, 32
    parties, being left out of,
        26–27, 31
    passion to break cycle, 25, 26–27
    perseverence to break cycle,
        24–25
    plays (theater), being left out of,
        24–25
    risk-taking to break cycle, 26–27
    setbacks, perseverence to offset,
        24–25
    stereotypes about being
        overweight, 18–19, 23, 24, 25

teachers' treatment of overweight
students, 23, 25
team sports, being left out of,
22–23
theater, being left out of, 24–25
See also family and overweight
members; overweight, under
happy; standards (impossible)
lifestyle change vs. dieting, 87–88
losing weight, 80–103
choices, making good, 86
cravings, 88, 93, 94–95
dieting caution, 88, 89
dietitian for help with, 80–81,
85–87, 88, 90
diets, tailored to individual
needs, 84
doctor for help with, 81, 85
encouragement for, 80, 82–84,
88–90, 96–97, 102
expectations (realistic) for,
101–103
family support for, 80, 82–84
fattening ingredients in meals, 86
friends' support for, 96–99, 102
help (professional) for, 77, 80–81,
82, 85–86
journal of foods eaten, keeping, 86
lifestyle change vs. dieting, 87–88
medical reasons for weight
problems, 85
metabolism impact, 62–63, 90
plateaus, 89–90
professional help for, 77, 80–81,
82, 85–86
success, 101–103
support for, 80, 82–84, 88–90,
96–97, 102
See also eating habits; exercise;
healthy diet rules

low-carb diets, 92–93
lunch, 91–92

M
mall rats, 28–30
masculine ideal (body), 37–40
mealtimes, eating well at, 90,
91–92
medical reasons for weight
problems, 85
metabolism, impact on weight,
62–63, 90
milk vs. soda, 91, 92, 93
models vs. real people, 32–33

N
name-calling about weight, 9,
13–15

O
obesity, 12
obsessive parents about weight,
50–52, 84
opinions of others, subjecting
yourself to, 24, 32
overeating, 63, 68–69, 70
overweight, under happy, 12–53
appearance, caring about,
29–30
clothes, shopping for, 28–30
covering up with clothes, 29, 35
defending your weight, 17, 18–19,
20, 45
differences in people and
romance, 42
discrimination about weight,
18–19, 20, 23, 24, 25
fantasies, romantic, 41–42
"fat" label, 9, 13, 14
feelings about, 9, 56

"flaws" in people and romance, 42
guilt feelings about, 18–19, 20
humor, using to your advantage,
    17, 20, 38–39
jokes about weight, 15–17, 18
labels, 9, 13–15
mall rats, 28–30
name-calling, 9, 13–15
obesity, 12
resources for, 104
responsibility for being overweight,
    19, 20
romance, 40–43
sexual identity, 40–43
shopping for clothes, 28–30
society values and, 19
stereotypes about being
    overweight, 18–19, 23, 24, 25
teasing about weight, 15–17, 18,
    20–21
verbal abuse about weight, 15–17,
    18, 20–21
visibility of weight, 12, 14
Web sites for, 104
See also causes of weight
    problems; eating habits;
    exercise; family and overweight
    members; healthy diet rules; left
    out (being); losing weight;
    standards (impossible)

P

parents, talking to about overweight
    issues, 46–49. *See also* family
    and overweight members
parties, being left out of, 26–27, 31
passion to break cycle of being left
    out, 25, 26–27
"perfect" girl or boy, 41–42

perseverence to break cycle of being
    left out, 24–25
physical activity. *See* exercise
physical changes during
    adolescence, 34–36, 39, 58–59
plateaus of weight loss, 89–90
plays (theater), being left out of,
    24–25
pop vs. milk, 91, 92, 93
portion sizes, 94
problems and weight gain, 74–77
professional help for losing weight,
    77, 80–81, 82, 85–86, 85–87,
    88, 90
protein, 90
puberty impact on bodies, 34–36, 39,
    58–59

R

realistic expectations for losing
    weight, 101–103
regular exercise, importance of, 74,
    99–100
resources for weight issues, 104
responsibility for being overweight,
    19, 20
restaurants, healthy eating, 92–93
risk-taking to break cycle of being
    left out, 26–27
role models, 33
romance, 40–43

S

salads, 91, 92
sandwiches, 91, 92
serving sizes, 94
setbacks, perseverence to offset,
    24–25
sexual identity, 40–43

shopping for clothes, 28–30

siblings and weight issues, 45

simple carbohydrates (sugar), avoiding, 91, 92, 93

smoothies, 93

snack foods, danger of, 69–70, 74, 75–76, 90, 92, 94

snacking (healthy), 92, 93

socializing and eating, 67

society values and weight, 19

soda vs. milk, 91, 92, 93

standards (impossible), 32–40

    adolescence impact on bodies, 34–36, 39, 58–59

    body changes during adolescence, 34–36, 58

    "curves," 34, 36

    feminine ideal (body), 24, 32, 34–36

    judgments of others, subjecting yourself to, 24, 32

    masculine ideal (body), 37–40

    models vs. real people, 32–33

    opinions of others, subjecting yourself to, 24, 32

    "perfect" girl or boy, 41–42

    puberty impact on bodies, 34–36, 39, 58–59

    role models, 33

    See also family and overweight members; left out (being); overweight, under happy

stereotypes about being overweight, 18–19, 23, 24, 25

success, losing weight, 101–103

sugar (simple carbohydrates), avoiding, 91, 92, 93

support for losing weight, 80, 82–84, 88–90, 96–97, 102

survival of ancestors, role of fat in, 61–62

T

talking to parents about overweight issues, 46–49

teachers' treatment of overweight students, 23, 25

team sports, being left out of, 22–23

teasing about weight, 15–17, 18, 20–21

theater, being left out of, 24–25

U

unconditional love from family, 44, 45, 48

V

variety of foods and overeating, 68–69, 74

vegetables, 93

verbal abuse about weight, 15–17, 18, 20–21

visibility of weight, 12, 14

W

Web sites for weight issues, 104

whole-grains, 91, 93

wild animals, internal signals to regulate hunger, 66

about the authors

Sylvie Boutaudou is a journalist who specializes in issues regarding science, health, and psychology.

Laëtitia Aynié is a painter and illustrator whose work has been seen on greeting cards, in children's books, and other media.

Melissa Daly is an associate editor at *Fitness*. She holds a degree in psychology from the College of William & Mary.